THE SUPERSTARS OF
BEVERLY HILLS
90210

By
Sara James

kidsbooks
Incorporated

Copyright © 1992 Kidsbooks, Inc.
7004 N. California Avenue
Chicago, IL 60645

ISBN: 1-56156-166-5

TABLE OF CONTENTS

Beverly Hills, 90210 is the People's Choice!

INTRODUCTION

Can't get enough of those babes from the hippest zip in town? You want to know more, more, more? Well, here it is!

Beverly Hills, 90210 is now in its third season, and hotter than ever! After a sizzling summer, most of the cast are finally seniors. Brandon, Brenda, Dylan, Kelly, Steve, Andrea, and Donna face exciting times filled with hopes and dreams, fears and anxieties, endings and beginnings. David studies hard to graduate early and also embark on life after high school.

The real life superstars of *90210* are also geared up for fabulous fun-filled times. Jason splashes onto the silver screen, while Shannen's *Obsession* is on the small screen. Brian stands firm on *Common Ground* and Luke rules the night with his "biting" success in the movies. Gabrielle keeps the home fires burning with her handsome new hubby, as Jenny engages herself to Dan for a lifetime of happiness. Tori remains true to her glamour gal image as she shops, shops, shops, then hits the town with hunky honey Ryan Ozar, and Ian has his eyes on new gal pal Suzanne Ircha.

Yes, changes are happening on screen and off, but one thing's for certain, your faves from those thrilling hills plan to make *90210* the longest-running, everlasting prime time TV show. And of course, they couldn't do that without you...their coolest, greatest, most devoted fans!

Jason Priestley scores another touchdown on *90210*.

CHAPTER ONE

JASON PRIESTLEY'S *CALENDAR GIRL*

Jason Bradley Priestley has been batting his baby blues into the homes of millions since he was four. Born August 28, 1969 in Vancouver, Canada, Jason got an early start in commercials and slowly worked his way into TV and small parts in the movies. "I thought I'd take my time and ease into it," jokes Jay.

The Jaybird has certainly eased his way into the hearts of his many fans as popular Brandon Walsh on *90210*. Jason is the show's quarterback and he's been throwing touchdowns every week for three years now. However, Jason realizes that having a hit show takes a team effort. "Everyone has to work together. That goes for the star down to the person who's running the craft service. Anything you can do to understand more about what everyone else's job is, it only helps," says Jason.

While he is very happy with his role, the show, and his friendship with his co-stars, the

Jaybird wants to stretch his wings and head on over to the big screen again. While Jason had small parts in the films, *Watchers*, *The Boy Who Could Fly*, and *No Where to Run*, he now has his first starring role in the flick *Calendar Girl.*

Set in a small town in Nevada in 1962, *Calendar Girl* is about three guys who have been friends since they met on the *Howdy Doody Show.* They've all been in love with the legendary Marilyn Monroe since they were 12, so they decide to travel to Hollywood to see if they can get a date with her!

Of Roy, the character Jason plays, he says, "He's hard to pin down. He's somewhat of a beatnik. He's got this very childlike quality. He does no editing whatsoever of what he thinks and what comes out of his mouth."

Roy's a boxer, and to get in shape for the role, Jay worked out with a punching bag at the gym. Like he could get in any better shape than he is already! Sounds like *Calendar Girl* is a sure winner!

Speaking of calendars, you're probably wondering what the Jaybird's social calendar looks like these days. Christine Elise is still Jason's best gal. The two are said to be a solid item. But don't despair, unlike the *90210* gals, Jay says marriage is a date he has yet to make!

Although temporarily tied down, Jason admits to liking all girls. "When it comes to love and girls, I find likeable things in every girl I meet. But more than anything, I love girls who are beautiful inside and out. Personality counts for me most."

And you can count on Jason to be coming into your homes for a long time to come!

Shannen Doherty is as beautiful as she is talented.

CHAPTER TWO

SHANNEN DOHERTY'S GOT THE STYLE

Shannen Maria Doherty knew what she wanted and what she liked as a very young girl. At the tender age of eight, she decided she wanted to be an actress, and although it took her two years to convince her parents, she was relentless.

Born in Memphis, Tennessee, on April 12, 1971, Shannen moved with her family to Los Angeles at age six. When the acting bug bit her at eight, she started to work in community theater. By ten, she had landed a guest role in *Father Murphy*, which led to a co-starring part in *Little House: A New Beginning*. Soon after that, Shannen played the leading role of Kris Witherspoon in the long-running, *Our House*.

A few years after *Our House* was canceled, Shannen won the part of Brenda on *Beverly Hills, 90210*. While the cast is made up of many talented actors and actresses, Shannen still manages to stand out. This year fans can find Shannen standing out in her new TV movie, *Obsession,* in which she plays the lead opposite veteran actor (*Knots Landing*) William Devane.

Shannen describes herself as, "confident, ambitious, fun, and very, very normal," and she has a style that's all her own. She's sophisticated, yet down to earth; beautiful, but wholesome; brainy, but uncomplicated; straightforward, yet warm.

"How does she do it?" you may ask. While most of it comes naturally, Shannen does work at presenting herself in different ways. Read on to find out more about the many sides of Shannen.

Shannen at Home

Shannen presently lives in a condo with her five dogs, but rumor has it that she and fiancé Chris Foufas just bought a $2 million home in, you guessed it, Beverly Hills. Shannen enjoys cozy evenings curled up with a good book or having dinner with friends.

When just hanging around home, Shannen likes to be real casual. Her favorite things to wear are big oversized shirts and sweaters, jeans and T-shirts. Of course, everything "caz" goes with her black leather motorcycle jacket. "I live in mine when I'm off the set!" says Shannen.

Shannen on the Set

Starring in a weekly TV show is a lot of work and Shannen is mostly business on the set.

"Being on the set 16 hours a day sometimes, I get stressed out," she says. "I don't want to be rude, so I go to my dressing room, put on some music, and call my girlfriends on the phone." When she's not chatting away, however, Shannen's hard at work on and off camera. She believes it's part of her job to care about her character. Shannen's really devoted to Brenda and likes to have a say in what Brenda does and says. Good for you, Shannen, it shows!

Shannen the Romantic

When Shannen wants to feel especially dreamy for Chris, she wears her beautiful brown locks down and gets decked out in something soft and flowy. Mellow colors like mauve and peach are perfect for times like this, and Shannen looks gorgeous in them. She keeps her makeup simple, she doesn't need much with her peaches and cream complexion, and finishes her face with her favorite mocha lipstick. Then she puckers up for a smooch with honey Chris.

Yes, there are many different sides to stunning Shannen, but one thing's for certain, she does it all with style!

Luke Perry arrives in style!

CHAPTER THREE

LUSCIOUS LUKE PERRY

Is he the shy quiet type, or is a silly guy lurking behind those dark brooding eyes? Is he a cool ladies man, or just a wild, crazy kind of guy? Luke Perry seems to be many things, the most of which is very, very popular!

Born Coy Luther Perry III in Mansfield, Ohio, Luke moved to the farming village of Fredricktown at age nine. Although he was the new kid in town, Luke is really outgoing, and quickly made friends.

Like most country boys, Luke was into bike riding, hunting, and fishing, and getting into a bit of trouble now and then. One year during high school he was lowered from a helicopter onto the school football field, in the middle of the game! But that's not all...he was dressed as Freddie Bird, the team mascot! Can you picture Luke in red feathers, funky yellow tights, a cape, and huge webbed feet?

Well, Luke was a hit as Freddie Bird and that incident was actually his first acting job. Once Luke discovered how much fun it was to entertain people, he wanted more. "I like to see people have a good time," says Luke.

Soon Luke was off to Hollywood, but unfortunately tinsel town was not ready for him...just yet. He moved to New York City and quickly landed the role of Ned Bates on the soap opera *Loving*. When Luke's *Loving* contract ran out, he headed back to LA, and this time the city was waiting for him. He landed the role of Dylan McKay almost as soon as he arrived.

Luke is fabulous as Dylan and that's because he really cares about his work. "I tend to put every bit of energy into acting," he says. And it shows.

Nowadays, Luke is branching out onto the big screen and is quite successful at that, too. His recent hit, *Buffy the Vampire Slayer*, was a tremendous success with his fans and his costars. Luke's director on *Buffy*, Fran Rubel Kazui, was also thrilled to be working with him. "He was very supportive of Kristy (Buffy) and me," recalls Fran. "He always started the day by giving both of us a big, warm hug."

Is Luke thinking about continuing to pursue his movie career? You bet he is. "It's not that I don't enjoy working on a TV show," says Luke. "In fact, I feel very lucky to have my job. It's just that, as an actor, I want to do the best work I possibly can for my fans, and I think I can achieve that goal better when doing films."

Films or TV, it seems like whatever Luke decides to do he'll be great at it, and adored by his fans!

CHAPTER FOUR

TORI SPELLING TALKS!

Tori Spelling grew up in the Hollywood spotlight. Born on May 16, 1973, she is the daughter of famous producer Aaron Spelling. Tori lived in the exclusive section of Bel Air, went to private schools, and hobnobbed with the stars. "When I was younger, my dad always took me to cast parties and affairs. I would meet the stars and it got me used to being around those types of people."

It came as no surprise then that Tori decided to become an actress. What was a surprise, however, was that Tori wanted to do it on her own. She has strong values, and was not a "spoiled rich kid." She knew that she wouldn't feel like she really accomplished anything if her parents just handed it to her. "My mom and dad never pushed me," says Tori. "It was more a case of they wanted for me what I wanted for me."

Today Tori has exactly what she wants. She loves playing Donna Martin on *Beverly Hills,*

Tori Spelling does it her way!

90210 and her character is extremely popular. Tori is growing as an actress and it's evident in the transition Donna has made since the beginning of the series. "I think with each character you play, you bring your own self into it. So I've made Donna less snobby. I don't like that—snobbiness."

Tori is true to her words. Seemingly unaffected by her exclusive Beverly Hills upbringing, Tori is a true friend and very close with her *90210* castmates. "Shannen and I have been very close since the pilot," says Tori and she claims that Gabrielle is like a big sister. "Gabrielle is very wise," she says. Tori loves to joke with Ian, "he makes me smile," and says Jason is "a really nice guy." Tori likes Luke because he's so caring and she says that, "Jennie is great."

But who is she closest to? You guessed it...Brian. "I love Brian. I think more than Shannen, I'm close to Brian because he plays my boyfriend, and we work together most. We're the same age, and we have the same friends and everything. We hang out off the set. He's just really cool."

Does this mean there's some offscreen romance? Sorry, Toribell doesn't mix business with pleasure. "I think Brian's very cute. I think out of all the guys I find him most attractive. Probably because we work together and do those (kissing) scenes. But we're too good of friends to— I mean, I've got a boyfriend."

Three gorgeous gals.

Two
handsome
hunks.

So who is this mystery man? His name is Ryan Ozar and he's not much of a mystery these days as Tori and he go out on the town together. Dating for about a year now, Tori met Ryan in LA, but now he's a sophomore at the University of Arizona as a business major. Besides the fact that Ryan is quite the cutie, Tori feels incredibly lucky to have him in her life. "He's totally unaffected by what I'm doing," she says. "I'm so lucky to have a boyfriend during this time period because if I didn't, I'd be scared to date because I'd be thinking, 'well does he like me for *me* or because I'm on the show?'"

Not to worry, Tori. It's obvious that anyone would like you for you!

Brian Austin Green dresses "GQ."

Brian Austin Green and partner Robb Boldt make up *Common Ground*.

CHAPTER FIVE

BRIAN AUSTIN GREEN'S ON *COMMON GROUND*

Brian started acting at age 10 and has been successful at it for quite some time now. Born July 15, 1973 in North Hollywood, California, Brian's first major role was as series regular Brian Cunningham on *Knots Landing*, where he literally grew up on-screen. Now as David Silver on *90210*, Brian is enjoying enormous popularity and has proven that he is one heck of a good actor.

However, acting was not Brian's first love. The son of famous drummer George Green, whose music can be heard on such shows as *The Simpsons*, Brian inherited his father's musical talent. In addition to playing the drums and piano, Brian has a wonderful voice and is the best hip-hop rap dancer on the set.

Through the years, Brian formed many musical groups, but none were really that serious. Until now that is! Brian has finally done it!

He's formed *Common Ground,* and Brian's so excited, he's ready to sing and dance...literally!

A while ago, Brian teamed up with Robb Boldt, a totally cute and very talented musician. Robb's been performing and touring with other musical acts for the past four years, but when he met Brian everything really came together. Robb is an unbelievable vocalist and can he write songs! Robb even produced the tracks for *Common Ground's* demo tape. How cool, he has a recording studio in his house.

Brian describes *Common Ground's* music as, "Hip-hop with very good melodies. It's very danceable...kind of like *Color Me Badd* and *Boyz II Men.*" This past summer, Brian and Robb made their first live appearance at Geauga Lake Amusement park just outside of Cleveland, Ohio. While Brian admits to having had stage fright, his fans would never know it because he was awesome. *Common Ground* performed "Faithful" and "Midnight Rain," two of their favorite songs, to the cheering and screaming of thousands of fans in the audience. Sounds like a major hit, for sure!

Brian and Robb hope to shortly sign *Common Ground* with a major record label and rumor has it that *90210* fans will get to see more of Brian's musical talents in the series' third year. The buzz is that Robb Boldt will have a recurring role as a student and will perform with Brian. Better stayed glued to the tube for this exciting happening.

Seems like Brian Austin Green's set sail on a steady course. With his acting career firmly in place, (you know he loves playing David Silver), and his music career in high gear, you're certain to be seeing lots more of Brian Green—the multi-talented performing machine!

Jennie Garth is simply beautiful.

CHAPTER SIX

SWEET AND LOVELY JENNIE GARTH

Of all the *90210* superstars, Jennie Garth is probably least like the character she portrays. Jennie is sweet and innocent, outdoorsy and down to earth—nothing like the stuck-up, snobby Beverly Hills socialite, Kelly Taylor. And her castmates agree.

"Jennie's great. She's like the opposite of her character. She's so sweet and fun. I don't know how she got cast. She told me that all her roles before this one were as stuck-up girls, too. I was going, 'How could you get those roles?' because she's so easygoing," says Tori. Luke describes her as, "sweetness."

Jennifer Eve Garth was born in Champaign, Illinois on April 3, 1972. She grew up on a 25 acre farm and is the youngest of John and Carolyn Garth's seven children. Jennie's family moved to Phoenix, Arizona when she was 13 and at first it was difficult for her to adjust to city life.

"I still miss the farm," says Jennie. "Growing up on a farm in such a tight family gave me incredible morals and values. I know it sounds hokey, but I feel like I'm a Walton."

Although leaving the farm was difficult for young Jenny, it enabled her to get more involved in dance, one of her great passions, and this eventually led to her acting career. Her dance instructor thought she should enter some talent pageants and it was at one of those pageants that Jennie was discovered by a Hollywood talent scout.

Jennie moved to LA after high school where she was quickly cast in the movie, *Teen Angel Returns*. She then won a role in the short-lived series, *A Brand New Life*.

When Jennie heard about the casting call for *Beverly Hills, 90210*, she tried her hardest to win the role of Kelly. It took her five auditions to nail it, and Jennie beat out several hundred competitors!

Now in year three of the series, Jennie is very comfortable playing Kelly and is making a "country" life for herself in tinsel town. Jennie owns a home which she shares with her two poodles, Zack and Sasha, and her kitten Roadie. She prefers hanging out with friends or frolicking in the park to attending gala celebrity events, anytime.

Jennie's best and only beau is fiancé Dan Clark, a happening drummer with the band,

Tongues & Tails. After dating just eight months, Dan popped the question and Jennie, "accepted in like three seconds," says Dan. Although the two have yet to set a wedding date, they spend as much time together as they can.

Jennie's idea of a perfect date is, "Taking the dogs and a picnic to the park." And if you think Jennie would be decked out for the occasion, think again. She's most comfortable in sneakers, jeans, and a tee with her beautiful hair pulled back in a ponytail.

It sure sounds like Jennie Garth is one sweet gal who's got it all...and she deserves it!

**Adventurous Ian Ziering was
at home on the water in Hawaii.**

CHAPTER SEVEN

ADVENTUROUS IAN ZIERING

"I was kind of a rambunctious kind of kid, you know, hyperactive," is the way Ian Ziering describes himself. And in fact, his adventuresome personality is the reason he wound up an actor.

Born Ian Andrew Ziering on March 30, twenty-something years ago, in Newark, N.J., Ian was a funny, hammy kid who always loved to be the center of attention. When he was four years old, a store manager suggested to Ian's mom that she get him into show business.

"I was running through the grocery store and my favorite thing was to knock a can off the shelf and roll it down the aisle. So I got caught and grabbed by the shoulders and they asked my name. Then they brought me to the front desk and announced, 'Will the mother of Ian Ziering come to the courtesy desk, your son is here.' So my mother comes to reclaim her son, and the store manager says, 'You know, you should get this kid into show business and let him expel some of this wild energy onstage.'"

Ian's mom took the advice. "She thought it might be interesting to see if I had an aptitude for it," says Ian. Although it took eight years for Ian to really get going, it was worth the wait!

While Ian had parts in the movie, *Endless Summer*, the Broadway show, *I Remember Mama*, and the soap opera, *The Guiding Light*, he led a normal life and attended local schools. He also continued his participation in sports. "I love athletics," says Ian. "I would have been on more school teams if I'd had the time. I would have played basketball and baseball."

Now that Ian's a superstar on one of the hottest shows, he's very busy with work, but in his free time he likes to be outdoors and active. "I'm really into keeping in shape." As if we hadn't noticed! "It's something I've always done to keep myself feeling good," explains the Z-man.

Recently, Ian spent some vacation time in romantic Hawaii where he participated in the Ritz-Carlton Mauna Lai Celebrity Sports Invitational, a fundraiser to benefit Project Eco-School, a non-profit environmental resource center. While there, the 6', 175 lb. hunky Ian played water sports like jet skiing as well as tennis and golf. You know Ian was successful at all these because he puts his heart behind all of that muscle!

Speaking of hearts, Ian's been seen around

town, and in heavenly Hawaii, with his new gal pal Suzanne Ircha. She's also blond, and beautiful, so the two make a divine couple! Could this be something serious? Only time, or Ian, will tell.

And only time will tell what's up next for Ian. Although he's incredibly happy on *90210* and would gladly stay there until he's a very old senior, the Z-man is always looking for excitement in his life. "I love doing challenging things — racing cars, bungee jumping," he says. So it only fits that this built-up guy would like to star in "an action adventure Indiana Jones-type of film in the future."

Sounds like an exciting future, for this adventuresome guy!

**Newlyweds Gabrielle Carteris and Charlie Issacs
are the picture perfect couple.**

CHAPTER EIGHT

GABRIELLE CARTERIS HAS IT ALL!

Gabrielle Carteris has always had a strong sense of family. She and twin brother Jimmy grew up in San Francisco under the close and watchful eyes of mother Marlene. A bright and bouncy child, Gabby was interested in dance early on and even performed with the San Francisco Ballet.

However, as fate would have it, Gabby never grew past 5'1" and her dance dreams were shattered. "There's not much call for short ballet dancers," she says. Never one to mope, Gabby switched to acting with the same passion she had applied to dance. There was one glitch to all this though. Mindful mother Marlene insisted that her daughter go to college. Way to go, mom!

So it was off to Sarah Lawrence College in New York, a short train ride from Broadway. Throughout college, Gabby landed some small roles on soaps and After School Specials, but it wasn't until 1990 that she hit it big...really big, as Andrea Zuckerman on *90210*.

Once again, Gabby threw herself into her work, and boy does it show. "Andrea has goals and is committed to making the world a better place," she says. "That's the way I grew up, too."

Gabrielle is true to her word. Recently, she attended a very special rally in Philadelphia. "The I Feel Great Show" is an annual event designed to motivate kids to lead a clean lifestyle—and go after their goals. "This is a program to really help educate young people and really support them in their choice to say no and feel good about it. It's about getting them going and feeling good about themselves. It's about having a sense of confidence," explains Gab.

It is just **that** sense of confidence that Gabrielle portrays in Andrea and which also led to her marriage to handsome hubby Charlie Issacs. Gabrielle always knew she wanted a career and a family, and was confident she could have them both!

Charlie and Gabrielle met when he was her stockbroker in New York and spent their first date eating sushi and going bowling. When Gabby moved to LA to film *90210*, Charlie moved too. He knew even then that he couldn't stand to be far away from her.

After two years of steady dating, Charlie popped the question at a candlelight dinner in romantic Hawaii. "There's something I want to ask you," said Charlie. "I want to know if you want to marry me." Gabrielle began to cry and said, "Yes." Charlie gave Gabby his grandmother's ring to seal their engagement.

On May 3rd Gabby walked down the aisle on brother Jimmy's arm to an instrumental version of "What a Wonderful World." She met hubby Charlie under the chuppa (a wedding canopy) where they exchanged vows in a traditional Jewish ceremony. Gabrielle wore a beautiful off-the-shoulder white gown and her bridesmaids wore silk chiffon. Among the 250 guests at the Four Seasons Biltmore Hotel in Santa Barbara, California were Gab's *90210* castmates (minus Shannen who was filming *Obsession).*

Gabby was absolutely glowing with happiness. "I really love him," said the blushing bride. What's Gabby's secret to a successful marriage? "You don't have to agree, you just have to listen," she says.

Looks like Gabrielle has got it all and is determined to keep it! Congratulations, Gabby!

The superstars of *Beverly Hills, 90210* are dressed up for a night on the town!

CHAPTER NINE

WHAT DO THEY SAY?

What do they say? Lots! Those great guys and gals from *Beverly Hills, 90210* speak out! If you listen closely, they'll tell all!

Tori Spelling on Luke Perry

"Luke's flirtatious. It's just his way. He's very...out there. But he's cool. I think he's probably the most like his character of any of us. He's very mysterious. Since the beginning, we've been very close so we talk and stuff. But he's not a very open person. He's very sensitive though, and he's very caring. But he doesn't show it a lot."

Tori Spelling on Kissing

"I'm still not comfortable with kissing scenes. They make me really nervous. Brian's the first guy I've ever kissed on TV or anything."

Shannen Doherty on Her Relationship With Chris

"We make time for each other. Because when everything is said and done, the acting may not be there, but the relationship will."

Shannen Doherty on Her Looks

"You know my eyes are a little off-center. Somebody pointed it out to me. I went, 'Really?' So I went home, and I looked in the mirror, and I said, 'Wow, they are.' And you know, to me, it's cool. It makes me different."

Jason Priestley on Fashion

"I'm different from most celebrities when it comes to clothes. I don't like to spend money on my wardrobe. I do like to shop in funky, second-hand stores, though."

Jason Priestley on Fan Mail

"We get letters saying, 'thanks for helping me.' And those letters really mean something, and they let you know we're making a difference. That's really what all of it is about."

Luke Perry on Fredricktown, Ohio

"Where I grew up, it looks like the movie, *Children of the Corn.* It does. You look outside and there's corn. And you look on the other side, it's okay because there's corn there, too. So, you know, you get to see a lot of corn where I'm from."

Luke Perry on Fame
"There's no more just walking down the street, and going somewhere, and hanging out with people. But it's the price you pay."

Brian Green on Growing Up
"If my parents weren't so morally straightforward, I think I would have had a lot more problems."

Brian Green on Being Forward
"I've never been shy. Even when I was a little kid, I was a real ham. I was the type of child who'd talk to complete strangers for no reason. If I was out for a meal with my parents, I'd run around to people in the next booth and introduce them to my whole family."

Ian Ziering on Life
"I blaze my own path."

Ian Ziering on His Favorite Meal
"My mom's chicken parmigiana with that wonderful spaghetti that she makes with it, and that incredible garlic bread. I'm not much on dessert, but my favorite is pecan pie, warm enough so that it melts the vanilla ice cream on top of it. Oh yeah!"

Jenny Garth on The Future
"Along down the line, I'd like to have a family and lots of animals."

Jennie Garth on Shopping

"I don't like to shop, so I power shop. I set aside time to go in and get everything that I need. I rush right through those shops and buy what catches my eye. I don't even care if it all fits, just as long as my shopping is done!"

Gabrielle Carteris on Hubby Charlie

"He's a good, good man. He's so loving and supportive. My best friend. I've never been happier. Everybody should be so lucky."

Gabrielle Carteris on Andrea Zuckerman

"I totally love this character. I love that she is smart and beautiful."

CHAPTER TEN

SPINOFF TO *MELROSE PLACE*

Since *Beverly Hills, 90210* is your absolute fave show, you're probably already addicted to its spinoff, *Melrose Place*. When gorgeous Jake Hanson (Grant Show) appeared on two episodes of *90210*, hearts were pounding, including Kelly Taylor's. So when the two decided to date, Kelly checked out Jake's digs on *Melrose Place*. That's when she, and you, met all of the great guys and gals who were Jake's friends and neighbors. They all live together in a Spanish style apartment complex in LA's trendy Melrose district. Although Kelly decided she was happier in the Hills, she discovered that *Melrose Place* was absolutely too cool! And so did you!

Do you need to know more? Of course! Here's a who's who on *Melrose Place*, *90210's* happening neighbors.

The stars of *Melrose Place*.

From left: Thomas Calabro, Josie Bissett, Grant Show, Amy Locane, Vanessa Williams, and Doug Savant.

Courtney Thorne-Smith and Andrew Shue.

Grant Show plays Jake Hanson

Jake is *Melrose's* Dylan McKay—the brooding silent type. Don't you love him already? He's a construction worker who's down on his luck, but struggling real hard to make it!

Actor Grant Show has made it! Best known as Officer Rick Hyde on the daytime soap, *Ryan's Hope*, Grant was born on July 30 in Detroit, Michigan. Raised in San Jose, California, Grant studied acting in London and performed on Broadway in *The Boys of Winter*. Jake may be *Melrose Place's* resident hunk, but Grant is very down to earth. "I'm not banking on what happened to Luke Perry for myself," he says. We'll see!

Amy Locane plays Sandy Louise Harling

Sandy Louise is a southern belle who uses her sweet voice and dynamite looks to get what she wants. A struggling actress, she waitresses at *Melrose's* Peach Pit, a hangout called Shooters.

Amy was born December 19 in New Jersey. At age 12, she started acting, and hasn't stopped. Her movie credits include, *Lost Angels* and *Cry Baby*, in which she starred opposite dreamy Johnny Depp. Lucky girl!

Andrew Shue plays Billy Campbell

Billy Campbell is an aspiring writer and really likeable kind of guy. He shares an apart-

*Beverly Hills, 90210
meets
Melrose Place.*

ment with Alison (just friends) and does odd jobs like teaching ballroom dancing and driving a taxi to pay the bills.

Like Billy, Andrew Shue graduated from college, but his major at Dartmouth was history, not writing. Born in Wilmington, Delaware, Andrew's birthday is February 20. Andrew was not always interested in acting. In fact, after college he went to Zimbabwe, Africa to play and teach soccer. However, upon his return, sister Elizabeth (*Cocktail, Adventures in Babysitting*) helped him get his start. The rest is *Melrose* history!

Courtney Thorne-Smith plays Alison Parker

Alison is a determined young woman with strong career goals. She's from the midwest and works as a receptionist in an advertising agency.

Courtney is also career-minded, about acting that is. Born November 8 in San Francisco, California, Courtney's been acting since high school. She's starred in the movies, *Revenge of the Nerds* and *Summer School.* She's also appeared in the series, *Day by Day, Fast Times at Ridgemont High, LA Law,* and *Anything But Love.* Courtney is very excited about *Melrose Place* and her fans are very excited about her!

Thomas Calabro plays Michael Mancini

Cute and caring Michael is newly married (only on the show) and a medical intern. He and wife Jane are also managers of the building they all share. A Chicago transplant, Michael is having a hard time adjusting to LA.

Thomas Calabro on the other hand is comfortable in LA as he has been acting there for some time now. Born in Brooklyn, New York on February 3, Tom has starred on the TV series, *Dream Street*, in the mini-series, *Vendetta*, and the made for TV movie, *Out of the Darkness*. However, Tom keeps close ties to his native New York and is a member of the prestigious New York Actors Studio and Circle Rep Lab. Tom's quite an actor and certain to shine on *Melrose Place*.

Josie Bissett plays Jane Mancini

Jane hopes to be a fashion designer someday, so she's learning about her trade by working in a trendy boutique. Very much in love with her adorable husband, Jane gets lonely when he has to put in so much time at the hospital.

Like her character Jane, beautiful blond Josie Bissett is also a newlywed, married to actor Rob Estes (*Silk Stalkings*). Born in Seattle, Washington on Oct. 5, Josie began her career as a fashion model in the U.S. and Japan. Josie has appeared in the films, *The Doors* and *Book of Love*, and on the TV shows, *The Hogan Family* and *Parker Lewis Can't Lose*. Jo can't believe her success at landing a part on *Melrose Place*. "It's still hard to believe sometimes that I make a living at what I do," she says. Believe it!

Doug Savant Plays Matt Fielding

Divine Matt is a social worker who runs a halfway house for runaways. He's a University of Southern California graduate and the resident do-gooder.

Doug Savant has been doing good in front of the camera for years. A southern California native, Doug was born on June 21 and started acting upon graduation from the University of California in Los Angeles. Since then, he has racked up a mondo list of acting credits. These include the movies, *Masquerade, Hanoi Hilton, Shaking the Tree*, among others. He also had appearances on the TV shows, *China Beach, Cagney and Lacey*, and *Knots Landing*. His fans are thankful they can now see Doug steadily on *Melrose Place.*

Vanessa Williams plays Rhonda Blair

Rhonda Blair is *Melrose's* nosy neighbor who teaches aerobic exercise and is trying to meet "Mr. Right." She describes her life as, "a series of cardio-funk classes interspersed with bad dates."

It's doubtful that Vanessa Williams has had a series of bad dates. How could she with her looks? Born in Brooklyn, New York on May 12, Vanessa is not the same Vanessa Williams of Miss America fame. What this Vanessa is famous for is her superb acting skills, which she has honed since age 11. A singer also, Vanessa has performed with the New York City Opera's Children's Chorus. Her acting credits include, *The Cosby Show*, the movie, *New Jack City*, and the broadway hit, *Sarafina*.

Now that you've been properly introduced to all the stars and characters, it's time for you to head on over to *Melrose Place*.

CHAPTER ELEVEN

TOTALLY AWESOME TRIVIA

You watch the show, you read all the gossip, but how much do you really know about the superstars of *Beverly Hills, 90210?* Take this totally awesome trivia test and find out!

1. How many carats is Shannen's engagement ring? *6.5*
2. What are the names of Jenny's two poodles? *back sacha*
3. What's the name of Ian's new gal pal? *Suzanne irc*
4. What do they grow a lot of in Luke's hometown of Fredricktown? *Corn*
5. What is the name of Brian's new group? *common of*
6. What song did Gabrielle walk down the aisle to? *what a wonderful world*
7. What's Tori's boyfriend's name? *Ryan ozal*
8. How many scars does Jason claim to have on his face? *13*

True or False

9. Jenny is engaged to be married? _✗_ T ___ F
10. Shannen's favorite food is Spanish. ___ T _✓_ F

11. Brian shares a house with his sister. ___ T ___ F
12. Jason's dating Christine Elise. ___ T ___ F
13. Luke is going out with Tori. ___ T ___ F
14. Gabrielle is the oldest cast member. ___ T ___ F
15. Ian pronounces his name "Eye-an." ___ T ___ F
16. Tori has five dogs. ___ T ___ F

Multiple Choice

17. Jennie's fiancé Dan plays in a band called a) Tongue & Tails b) E Street Band c) Hip Zippers d) none of the above
18. Ian's new gal pal is a) Betty b) Brenda c) Suzanne d) Christine
19. Brian's musical partner is a) Robin Thicke b) Robb Boldt c) Jason Priestley d) Hammer
20. Who are the cast's practical jokers? a) Ian and Jason b) Jennie and Tori c) Tori and Shannen d) Luke and Jason
21. Tori's favorite color is a) black b) white c) red d) blue
22. On their first date, Gabrielle and Charlie went a) bowling b) to the movies c) ice skating d) to the Emmy Awards
23. Luke's potbellied pig is named a) piggy b) Fred c) Jerry Lee d) John Wayne
24. The character Jay plays in *Calendar Girl* is named a) Bob b) Roy c) Charlie d) Jay

FILL IN THE BLANKS

25. Luke starred in the recent release _Buffy_, *the Vampire Slayer.*
26. Gabrielle's wedding ring was passed down from Charlie's _grandma_.
27. Tori auditioned under the name of Tori _Michele_
28. Brian's favorite hair color for girls is ~~red~~ _red_
29. Ian visited the state of _Hawii_ during the summer of '92.
30. In LA Shannen shops at _Fred Segal_.
31. Jennie's favorite color is _red_.
32. Jason pays an aspiring ~~Boy~~ _Boxer_ in *Calendar Girl.*

(See Page 64 for Answers)

Tori says that
Ian makes her laugh.

Luke and Gabrielle
first met in New York
when they were
starting out.

CHAPTER TWELVE

90210 PUZZLE POWER

Beverly Hills Jumble

Can you unscramble the following words to discover the message the superstars of 90210 have for you?

OINJ SU ORF URO BUOFALSU IRNESO RYEA.
EES OUY EHTRE!

(See Page 64 for Answers)

Join us for our fabulous
Senior year, see
you there.

What's In A Name?

How many words can you make from the name Gabrielle? Can you find at least 30?

Gabrielle

Gabe	Gab
Gabie	bag
I	rabi
A	rabie
Gabrielle	bee
ill	tol
lie	real
Bag	reel
Bagie	rail
Bell	rale
Billie	rag
Gail	grab
ball	brag
lab	leg
Big	girl

All Scrambled Up

Jennie's mixed up her words. Can you help her unscramble them and find out more about her?

TRETPY *pretty*

NMIALA VLERO *animal lover*

RMFA LRIG *farm girl*

NGEGDEA *engaged*

DCNAER *dancer*

(See Page 64 for Answers)

Shannen looks super in leather.

Jason takes his dog Jeff for a walk.

90210 Word Search

Can you find the first names of the superstars of *90210* in the word search puzzle below? Look up, down, backward, forward, and diagonally.

Jasoñ   Shannen
Luke   Jennie
Ian   Gabrielle
Brian   Tori

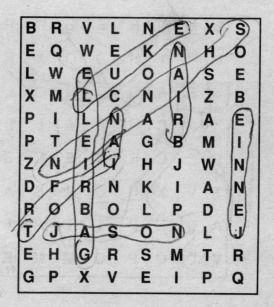

(See Page 64 for Answers)

Let's Zig Zag

The following words that are associated with the show *90210* are hidden in the puzzle below. Look closely now. These words twist in all directions.

Peach Pit ~~Peach Pit~~
Porsche ~~Porsche~~
School ~~School~~
Beach ~~Beach~~

Blond ~~Blond~~
Homework ~~Homework~~
Date ~~Date~~
Music

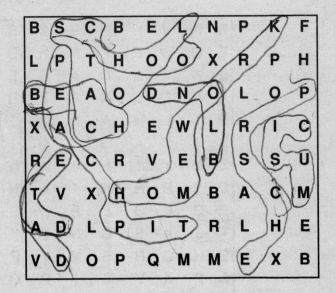

(See Page 64 for Answers)

The Sizzling Summer of '92!

Do you remember all the exciting things that happened during the summer of '92? Test your brainpower by completing the puzzle below.

Down

1. In what French city did Brenda and Donna spend six weeks?
4. Who was Kelly interested in during the summer?
5. Steve won the volley_____ tournament.
8. _____'s parents got back together again.

Across

2. Brandon worked at the _____ club.
3. Kelly's mom gave birth to a baby ____.
6. What other character worked with Brandon?
7. In France, Donna was discovered as a _____.

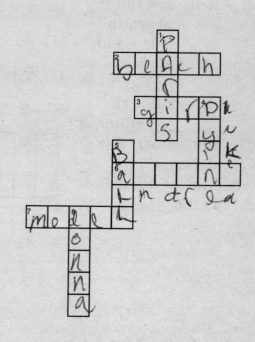

(See Page 64 for Answers)

61

Get Crossing!

Complete the puzzle below to find out more about your favorite characters.

Down

1. Kelly's mom's new married name is _____.
3. All the characters attend _____ Beverly High.
4. Brandon and Brenda's last name is _____.
7. Kelly used to date _____.

Across

2. In one episode, Kelly met the musical group _____ Me Badd.
5. Steve's mom is an _____.
6. Brandon is the _____ editor of the school newspaper.
8. The local hangout is the _____ Pit.

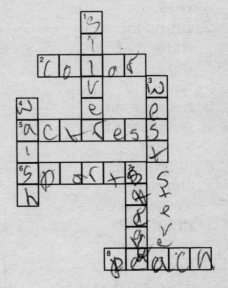

(See Page 64 for Answers)

Secret Message

Use the chart below to decode a special message from the superstars of *Beverly Hills, 90210*.

4-15-14'-20   6-15-18-7-5-20   20-15

23-1-20-3-8   15-21-18   19-16-9-14-15-6-6

19-8-15-23,   13-5-12-18-15-19-5   16-12-1-3-5.

1	2	3	4	5	6	7	8	9	10	11	12	13	14	15	16
A	B	C	D	E	F	G	H	I	J	K	L	M	N	O	P

17	18	19	20	21	22	23	24	25	26
Q	R	S	T	U	V	W	X	Y	Z

(See Page 64 for Answers)

DONT (Forget) to watch)

OU ((SPINOFF/SHOW)

MELROSE place

ANSWERS

Totally Awesome Trivia
1. 6.5; 2. Zack and Sasha; 3. Suzanne Ircha; 4. Corn; 5. *Common Ground*; 6. "What a Wonderful World"; 7. Ryan; 8. 13; 9. T; 10. F; 11. T; 12. T; 13. F; 14. F; 15. T; 16. F; 17. a; 18. c; 19. b; 20. d; 21. c; 22. a; 23. c; 24. b; 25. Buffy; 26. Grandmother; 27. Mitchell; 28. Red; 29. Hawaii; 30. Fred Segal; 31. Red; 32. Boxer

90210 Word Search

Get Crossing:

Let's Zig Zag:

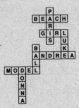

Beverly Hills Jumble:
Join us for our fabulous senior year. See you there!

All Scrambled Up:
Pretty; Animal lover; Farm girl; Engaged; Dancer.

Secret Message:
Don't forget to watch our spinoff show, *Melrose Place*.

The Sizzling Summer of '92!:

$2.95 US
$3.50 Can

THE SUPERSTARS OF
BEVERLY HILLS
90210

They are the reigning kings and queens of primetime TV! They star on one of the most popular shows on television today! They are the hottest, the coolest, the cutest, and most awesome . . . they are the superstars of *Beverly Hills, 90210*!

In this new book get up-to-the-minute info about Jason, Shannen, Luke, Jenny, Ian, Gabrielle, Brian, and Tori plus fabulous full-page photos. Also, test your trivia skills and puzzle power w~~ith~~ exciting *90210* brainteasers.

This publication was not authorized o~~r~~ the producers of *Beverly Hills, 90210* or a~~ny~~

ISBN 1-56156-166-5

UPC
0 40296 00166 4

kidsbooks
Incorporated